MAKE EXTRA MONEY ONLINE BY JANE FAZACKARLEY

Copyright: Jane Fazackarley.

Disclaimer: All of this information was correct at the time of writing. I do not make claims that anyone can make a fortune working from home and I cannot accept responsibility for any of the companies listed. Before beginning any opportunity, it is wise to do an Internet search to see what other people are saying about them before signing up. It is also wise to keep your anti-virus up-to-date before visiting sites or downloading software. The author accepts no liability for any damage or loss.

Introduction

The Internet has given rise to a wide range of opportunities for people to earn some extra money at home.

There are plenty of scams out there, but there are also plenty of genuine companies that offer the opportunity to earn some extra money online.

Listed in this book are a number of companies who all offer ways of making money. These opportunities aren't designed to give a full time income, but to offer ways of earning some extra money.

Some ways of earning will work better for some people than they do for others, but with a wide range to choose from there should find something suitable for most people.

With the exception of the sales/party/plan section, I've only chosen companies that don't ask for sign up fees. Included in this guide are both US and UK opportunities.

What You'll Need:

Internet Access

PayPal account and Checking/bank Account

Google AdSense account for some of the writing opportunities

Taxes

You'll be working for a lot of these companies on a self-employed basis and will be liable for declaring any extra income earned from these opportunities. Ask the HMRC for advice before starting.

Further information on self-employment is available at:

http://www.hmrc.gov.uk/selfemployed/

For details on self-assessment, visit:

http://www.hmrc.gov.uk/selfemployed/register-selfemp.htm

In the US, visit:

http://www.irs.gov/Businesses/Small-Businesses-&-Self-Employed/Self-Employment-Tax-(Social-Security-and-Medicare-Taxes)

NOTES

Survey Sites

Some people love survey sites, while other people hate them. Survey sites cannot be relied upon for a regular income, but it is possible to earn some extra money from completing surveys.

Your earnings will also depend on your profile; the more detail added to your profile, the more chance you have of getting surveys.

There are pros and cons with taking surveys. The positives are that you can earn cash and sometimes get free products to test while the downside is surveys aren't sent out on a regular basis and people can get part way through a survey only to find they've been screened out. Surveys can also be time consuming.

Read the many reviews online before joining a survey site and see which ones are best suited to you. Personally, I don't do surveys that are too lengthy, and choose survey sites with a low minimum pay-out or that are well-established and have a good reputation. There

There are many more survey sites than the ones I have listed; it is just a matter of finding the right ones for you.

Global Test Market

This US company pays its members once they have reached the 1,000 points threshold which is equal to $50.00. I signed up a while ago and they do sent regular surveys, but what people earn will vary as it depends on how many surveys a participant qualifies for. Some surveys only pay in sweepstakes entries, but there is no obligation to complete those, and users of the site can just complete the surveys that reward points. To register visit: https://www.globaltestmarket.com/join.php

Opinion Outpost

Opinion Outpost is another US-based company. Opinion Outpost offer pay-outs via PayPal or users can redeem their points for other rewards. The site also offers cash prizes or the points earned can be used to donate the cash equivalent to charity. The sign up form is short, unlike some other sites, so the sign up process is quick and straight forward. http://www.opinionoutpost.com/

Vocalabs

This company offers surveys both online and over the phone and they are seeking views on customer service standards. Surveys are open to residents in the US and Canada; the company pays via PayPal. The surveys pay 0.50 cents to $1.00, but more detailed surveys usually pay more. http://www.vocalabs.com/panelist/index.jsp

Crowdology

The Crowdology research community is open to residents in the UK aged sixteen years or over. Payments are made via PayPal once registered members have earned £4.00. Pay-outs for surveys vary from 40 pence - £10 a time. To register, visit the site at:

http://www.crowdology.co.uk/Register.html

Valued Opinions

Valuedopinions.co.uk is open to UK residents and has 40,000 members in the UK. They pay users in vouchers and users qualify for payments once they have reached the £10 level; a voucher will then be sent to the registered address. Awards vary from survey to survey and from experience I can say that survey invitations are quite regular.

Valued Opinions also has a site for US users and surveys pay $1-5 a time. Once users have accumulated $20, then they will become eligible to receive a gift card.

www.valuedopinions.co.uk/join/

http://www.valuedopinions.com/

Ipsos IPanel

This site pays out in vouchers once a participant has accumulated enough points. Unlike some sites, Ipsos usually give at least some points even if the user doesn't qualify for the full survey - and the points all add up. There are a number of vouchers to choose from and Ipsos has proven to be reliable at sending our rewards when requested. A lot of people prefer sites that pay cash but vouchers can be just as valuable.

YouGov

YouGov are a UK-based site offering surveys. YouGov pay in points which can then be covered into cash. Payments are made via cheque once the £50 payment limit has been reached, the equivalent to 5000 points. Some people reach the pay-out easier than others. Like most survey sites, it all depends on the profile and how many surveys the user qualifies for.

www.yougov.co.uk

Survey Savvy

Survey Savvy pays it users for completing surveys. Users of the site can also earn from their referrals. Users qualify for a payment once they've earned $1 and the payment will be mailed by check. The site also offers cash prizes and members of the site have the chance to enter sweepstakes for prizes of $500. Find out more at: www.surveysavvy.com

American Consumer Opinion

American Consumer Opinion has been about for a while now. Once you've signed up to the site, you'll have the opportunity to take part in product evaluations and surveys. Participants earn points for each survey completed and each point is worth a penny. Once users have reached 100 points they cash out via PayPal. This site is based in the US, but it is open to International users.

http://www.acop.com/

Just the Answer

This is a UK-based site which offers quiet regular surveys. They pay in answer points which can be exchanged for either Amazon vouchers or the points can be donated to charity. Points can also be used to enter prize draws. I get offers of surveys from this site and they seem quite active. I also find that Amazon vouchers come in useful for paying for presents or household items.

http://portal.justtheanswer.co.uk/communities/default.aspx?p=p592785398&n=%280%3a0-881377263%230%2c+690%29

My Survey

They offer a variety of rewards for taking part in surveys including vouchers and PayPal payments. I used to be a member of this site when they were still called Lightspeed. However, I have not taken part for a while and have now re-registered with them as I found they offered regular surveys - which paid up to £3.00 - and they are quick at paying via PayPal.

UK.mysurvey.com/

NOTES

11

MYSTERY SHOPPING

Getting paid to shop might sound like a dream come true for some people – and it is perfectly feasible with mystery shopping. It is true that people can get free meals and haircuts, but mystery shoppers must be careful and follow the guidelines. Shoppers are usually given a budget and can claim the money back when they have completed the task. However, if the task is not completed to the standards required, then the mystery shopper will run the risk of not being paid, and that is why I stayed away from those kind of tasks.

I did get paid and my money refunded for buying skin care products, a £10.00 supermarket shop, some fast food meals, and all sorts of other opportunities; I used to sell my free gifts to make some extra money that way. Phone calls can pay up to £4.00 and usually take two minutes, while other shops can pay anything from £5.00 upwards.

Mystery shoppers will get a mileage allowance and when I was working as a mystery shopper I used to get paid for bus fare.

Before undergoing a mystery shop, a mystery shopper will have to undergo training for the task, which is often done online. Results are usually entered online or by phone and mystery shops can be carried out as visits, phone calls, or a company might want to use your mailing address in return for a vouchers.

The work is irregular, so I found it couldn't be depended on for income. The kind of work - and how often the work is offered - will depend on you profile.

Remember to carry out your mystery shopping task exactly as directed or you might not get paid. You'll have to have a pretty sharp memory and good observation skills as well as you'll often be expected to remember names and descriptions of the people who served you.

It is often advised that a mystery shopper fills out the details of their visit as soon as possible, but don't do this where you could be seen by a member of a staff as they are not supposed to know you are a mystery shopper.

Market Force

Market Force is a US-based mystery shopping company looking for independent contractors to take part in assessments of fast food stores, gas stations, grocery stores and more. In return for the work, mystery shoppers receive a payment for each job. Mystery shoppers often get to keep any purchases and have the chance for free meals if they are assessing a fast food chain or restaurant. Theatre checking and merchandising assignments are also available, but you'll need to sign up separately for this.

http://www.marketforce.com/become-a-mystery-shopper.

ACE

ACE is based in MO and is inviting applications for mystery shopping work. To sign up, applicants need to go to the 'become a mystery shopper' link, which is on a red box to the left of the home page. Once the form has been filled out and the application has been accepted, then you'll be added to their database of shoppers.

The National Shopping Service

The National Shopping Service is based in the United States and are currently inviting applications. The kind of work offered includes airlines, hotels and stores. The company also carry out audits. Payments for mystery shopping jobs are sent via check. The application form is available at:

http://www.nationalshoppingservice.com/public/mystery _shopper_registration.asp

GFK US

GFK US requires mystery shoppers for a range of assignments. I used to work for the UK office and found them a good company to work for and they offered me the most work. They offer training both before starting work for them and also offer specific training for individual assignments. Mystery shoppers can choose to be notified via email when work becomes available. The US site is at:
https://www.gfkmysteryshops.com/GfK.smart.SASSIE/

The UK site is at: http://www.gfkmysteryshopping.co.uk/

When I worked for the UK site, the payments used to made via bank deposit, but I noticed that the US site offer PayPal as a payment option.

Customer Perspectives

Customer Perspectives are looking for mystery shoppers. Shoppers will get paid via PayPal once they have completed their shop. Rates of pay weren't stipulated on the site, but these will vary from job to job. The application form is available here:

http://lazarus.archondev.com/cp/shoppers.nsf/InternalNavFrameset?OpenFrameSet&Frame=WorkspaceFrame&Src=%2Fcp%2Fshoppers.nsf%2Fshopperapp%3FOpenForm%26AutoFramed

You Count On Us

You Count on Us are inviting applications for mystery shoppers in the US. They state that mystery shopping jobs could pay $10-$100. From my own experience with mystery shopping, the fees you'll be paid depend on the complexity of the job: the more complex, the more you get paid. To find out more about the company - and to find the application form - visit:

http://www.ucountonus.com/newsite/index.php

Retail Active

Retail Active is based in Oxford, UK and are currently seeking people to work as mystery shoppers and assessors. Jobs might include assessing banks, hotels, supermarkets and pubs. Mystery shoppers will be given full training before starting work.

http://www.retailactive.com/mystery_shopping.aspx

Shopper Anonymous

Shopper Anonymous is based in the UK are currently looking for mystery shoppers. The application consists of a short form, which is available on the website. Types of visits include farm shops, holiday attractions, supermarkets and garden centres. The application form is available by clicking the following link: http://www.shopperanonymous.co.uk/apply-to-become-a-mystery-shopper/

Performance in People

Performance in People is based in the UK and offer a wide range of mystery shopping work to successful applicants. The work offered includes covert mystery shopping, report-based shops and telephone mystery shopping. They also offer email mystery shopping and require postal addresses to send mail to, which usually pays by means of a gift voucher.
http://www.performanceinpeople.co.uk/contact/become-a-mystery-shopper.php

TNS

TNS are based in the UK and offer mystery shopping work. From experience, the whole application process is rather lengthy and I had actually forgotten I had applied. However, this was a while ago and the application process may now be a lot swifter. It was months before I head back from them and began to get offers for work, so don't be surprised if TNS don't get in touch straight away. To get started, applicants need to fill out the online application form and complete a quiz before they can get started.

http://www.tnsglobal.com/work-for-us/mystery-shopper

Retail Eyes

Retail Eyes are looking for UK-based mystery shoppers. The application form is available online and is straight forward to fill out. Mystery shoppers need to be over 18, have a computer with Internet access, a scanner, digital camera and a printer. They state that jobs pay £5-10 each. You'll find the 'Become a Shopper' link on the left of the page: http://uk.marketforce.com/home/

NOTES

18

TRANSCRIPTION WORK

If your aim is to work as a transcriptionist from home then you'll need to have a fast typing speed. Most companies require typists to have a typing speed of 75 words per minute; some ask for less at around 55 words per minute. Typists will also need audio equipment such as a foot pedal to make typing quicker and easier, and you'll need to have a reliable broadband Internet service, but to start with typists may be able to download software online for transcribing such as Total Recorder for listening to files

I have done some transcription work, but I found it to be very tough on my wrists and shoulders due to the repetitive nature of the work, so this is something that should be taken into consideration before undertaking this kind of work. Also, the hours can be very odd, so this is something else to bear in mind.

Companies like Scribie, Transcribe Me and Quick Tate might be better suited for the beginner as the audio files are much shorter. Transcribe Me files are usually less than a minute long; when I did some work for them each piece was paying around five cents. I didn't need any special equipment or to download any software so Transcribe Me might be a good option for starting out and to test out if transcription work is suitable. I have heard good things about Scribie, but do not currently work for them. Their application process is rather long; when I applied there was a waiting list of more than 200 days.

Mechanical Turk is also a good way of picking up short pieces of transcription work and for building experience.

If typing work in general appeals then advertising locally might be one way of getting work - and it has worked for me in the past. Searching freelance sites for similar work is also another option.

Global Transcription Services

Global Transcription Services are based in the UK and are seeking transcriptionists to work from home. If a potential employee doesn't have the equipment required to carry out the work, then the site details some free software that can be downloaded. You'll need to read the guidelines carefully before applying and you'll have to carry out a typing test first. Payments are made via bank transfer or by PayPal. http://www.global-transcription-services.co.uk/transcriptionists-guidelines.html

Alphabet Secretarial

Alphabet Secretarial carry out legal, medical, conference and academic transcription. Anyone interested in working for them needs to fill out a short form online and send a copy of your CV. They advise applicants that if they haven't heard within a week to presume that the application has been unsuccessful.

http://www.alphabetsecretarial.co.uk/work-for-us

Pioneer Transcription Services

Pioneer Transcription Services are based in the US and have openings for general and legal transcriptionists. They have an application form available online and they seem to accept UK applicants as well. There is more information available at: http://www.pioneer-transcription-services.com/transcriptionjobs.html

Ubiqus

Ubiqus has many openings including requirements for translators, interpreters, summary writers and transcriptionists. They are based in the United States, they do, however, employ people from the United Kingdom, as I have previously undergone training with them. Application forms are available online and they just require some basic information including details of any previous experience.. http://www.ubiqus.com/GB.htm

Scribie

Scribie is a good option for starting out in transcription as they have shorter files which need to be typed up, usually less than six minutes. They pay $10 per hour of audio and it is a good way of gaining experience for people new to transcription work. There are also bonuses for every three hours completed in a month. Payments are made via PayPal. There is a lengthy wait before applicants can undergo the test they'll need to carry out before being offered work. To find out more go to http://scribie.com/ and click on the 'work for us' link, which can be found at the top right hand corner of the page.

Transcribe Me

I've recently discovered a site called Transcribe Me. This is also a good company for beginners and they have a simple test that has to be completed before starting work. The application form is short and sweet so it doesn't take long to set up an account with them. You'll need to have Chrome downloaded on your computer. From what I can tell this is a new site so there are not too many reviews around. http://transcribeme.com/transcriber-careers

Quicktate

Quicktate need transcriptionists to type up voice mail messages, letters and memos etc. They expect people to already have their own equipment and they are looking for people who already have experience with transcription work. There's a short application form for people to fill out before they can get started and applicants will need two references. Applicants also need to read several documents and agreements before they can start:

http://typists.quicktate.com/transcribers/signup

NOTES

Miscellaneous

Whether it is carrying out short tasks or working as a virtual assistant, there are plenty of ways to make money online. Some people like the variation of working for short task sites like Mechanical Turk while others like steadier opportunities such as customer service work.

It all depends on what suits you and the kind of extra money you are looking to earn.

Mechanical Turk

Amazon owned Mechanical Turk pay people for completing tasks. The pay varies from extremely low at a cent or 2, but workers can earn considerably more for certain tasks. Article writing and surveys can pay $4-6 dollars and if you know a subject well then you could easily write four 3-400 word articles in an hour. Pay is via transfer to your bank account if you're in the US or in Amazon.com credits if based in the UK. I have often used my money to buy stock from Amazon and sell it on so I convert my Amazon gift card balance into cash that way.

https://www.mturk.com/mturk/welcome

Gig Walk US/Canada

Gigwalk is open to residents of US and Canada and pays people for carrying out a range of tasks such as mystery shopping, photography or interviewing a band. Applicants will need to own a smartphone for completing tasks. Payments are made once independent contractors have earned at least $35.00 and as with other sites, workers are responsible for their own taxes. Find out more at: http://gigwalk.com/

Caption Matrix

I discovered Caption Matrix when I was looking for transcription work. Caption Matrix has several vacancies available for US, Canadian and International applicants. The work involves transcribing video footage, proofreading video transcription or working as a video caption specialist. Applicants need to have a Gmail account for this and you'll need to follow the application process carefully as resume/CVs without the correct information in the subject line won't be accepted. http://www.captionmatrix.com/job-openings

Taskrabbit US ONLY

Taskrabbit is another US-based company. The site has many tasks on offer such as dog walking or putting together furniture. However, it is not open to every state. To become a "taskrabbit", applicants must first join the site and apply, and then take part in a video interview. Next, the company will run a background check on the applicant; the applicant will then receive a handbook, and then they'll be ready to start work on Taskrabbit.

https://www.taskrabbit.com/become-a-taskrabbit

Do My Stuff US ONLY

Do My Stuff is open to residents in the US. Users of the site can outsource the tasks that need doing such as dog walking, cooking dinner, shopping etc. When someone completes the task, they can earn a fee for carrying out the work. Unfortunately, when I checked I could not get the FAQ to work properly so I could not find out how payments were made. http://www.domystuff.com/index

Field Agent US ONLY

Field Agent is another US-based company. Once signed up, people can carry out various tasks using their phones. The work includes price checks, audits, photography, mystery shopping, surveys etc. Payments are made via PayPal and tasks pay between $3-12.00 each. Anyone wishing to undertake work will need to download an app in order to do so. Find out more at: http://www.fieldagent.net/faq-agent/

Fancy Hands US ONLY

Fancy Hands aren't recruiting at the time of writing, but I felt this company was worth including. Again they are based in the US; they require people to work as virtual assistants. The application process is quite extensive and will involve interviews and tests, and if passed your application should be accepted. http://www.fancyhands.com/faq

Crowdflower

Crowdflower is a crowdsourcing site that requires its users to carry out short tasks. The site states that it has outsourced 800 million micro tasks. The sign up process is simple and workers can start earning straight away if there is suitable work available. http://crowdflower.com/channel

Clickworker

Clickworker has a range of short tasks for homeworkers to complete and a low pay-out of $10 which shouldn't be too hard to achieve. Work includes translation, writing, research etc. Anyone wishing to take part must first complete a few assessments and you'll be offered work based on the results.
http://www.clickworker.com/en/clickworker?customer=false

6336.com

6336.com pay people to answer questions via text. When I looked the vacancies were closed. However, when vacancies become available the company will say so via their Twitter feed. I know a few people who do well with companies like this so it worth keeping a check on when work becomes available. You'll find more information by visiting their site at:
http://www.aqa.63336.com/vacancies.htm

Fiverr

If you have a talent then you can put it to good use on Fiverr and earn $5.00 for efforts, minus $1.00 for commission. Once you've registered with Fiverr, freelancers can decide which skills they'd like to offer; there are plenty of categories to choose from. It could be web design, artwork, advertising, writing blog posts, SEO articles, transcription, or translation etc.

www.fiverr.com

Virtual Assistants

Virtual Assistants provide office support for companies such as handling calls, typing letters etc. These types of companies have become increasingly popular and it is possible to earn well at this. You'll find many agencies listed online.
http://www.virtualassistants.co.uk/Become-A-Virtual-Assistant.htm

Virtually Sorted

Virtually Sorted is another company offering virtual assistant work from home. Workers have to be available to work 20 hours a week, have Microsoft Office installed, attend meetings via phone and pass the tests set out. Anyone interested can find further details by going to:
http://www.virtuallysorted.com/contact-us/i-want-to-be-a-va/

Slice the Pie

Slice the Pie is a music review site. Its primary aim is to give honest reviews to bands and solo artists for their material. A lot of the artists featured on the site are just starting out so fair and honest feedback is valuable to them. As a bonus, the site also pays for reviews.

Reviewers get a base rate which is between 1-3 cents and a bonus amount for each review which can be between 8 cents - 41 cents. This is a steady earner and I've earned over a few hundred dollars so far. Payment is made via PayPal once a reviewer has reached $10.00.

Jingit US ONLY

Jingit is available to residents in the US. Users have to download an app that enables them to make money through cash back offers. Users of the site also have the opportunity to earn extra money through watching videos and giving feedback on them. Earnings are paid through the music.me service or via a Jingit Debit card. Find out more at: https://www.jingit.com/home/how-jingit-works/

Idea Connection

If you have the ability to solve a company's problems, then you could earn yourself some extra cash with Idea Connection. Problem solvers could earn anything from $2,000 upwards. The problems aren't listed on the site, instead users must sign up and give details of their expertise and then they will be contacted when a project comes along that matches their skills. The site also has Idea Rallies, and offers the opportunity to earn through sourcing technologies and through research work. http://www.ideaconnection.com/solve-problems.html

Liveworld

Liveworld currently has vacancies for moderators to work from home. Content would include forum posts, videos, pictures and audio files. To apply, you need to be a social media "super-user" and have previous experience in moderation. It is easy to gain experience in moderation work as many websites look for voluntary moderators, so the required experience can be gained that way.

http://www.liveworld.com/careers/liveworld-moderator/

Innocentive

Innocentive uses crowdsourcing to solve problems. Unlike Idea Connection, they do list the problems that companies need solving on the site. When I checked there were projects for creating turbo chilling containers and self-monitoring for heart failure patients, among many other challenges that need solving. Prizes of $1,000 upwards are offered.
https://www.innocentive.com/about-innocentive

Epinions

Epinions pays people for product reviews on everything from books to cars. In order to earn all you need to do is submit a product review about something you own or have used and submit it. Writers earn through income share and US residents can cash via PayPal once they've earned $5.00.

http://www.epinions.com/?sb=1

1-800 Flowers US ONLY

At the time of writing, 1-800 Flowers were looking for people to work from home as Customer Service Representatives. The vacancies advertised were to help assist over Mother's Day. However, they sometimes have openings at other times of the year so it is worth keeping a look out on their employment opportunities page to see what they have available at any given time.
http://ww31.1800flowers.com/template.do?id=template8&page=9000&conversionTag=true

Teletech@home US ONLY

Teletech@home recruits people from across the United States to work at home as a customer care associate. You'll need to read through the full lists of terms and conditions to ensure that you meet of all of the company's requirements so that you can carry out the work from home. Find out more about the company by reading the FAQ section:
http://www.hirepoint.com/athome-en-US/

Humanatic

Humantic need people to listen into calls and to make an assessment. I've read various reviews on the company and it seems that the workload can vary from person to person, but the reviews are largely positive. Workers also have to chance to earn extra through bonuses. Payments are made once the user has made $5.00; payments are made via PayPal. I did try signing up with them, but it wouldn't accept my phone number so perhaps they only accept applicants from the US, but it is worth a look.
http://www.humanatic.com/pages/tour.cfm

CloudCrowd

CloudCrowd offers short tasks such as article writing and editing. There is usually plenty of work available, however, applicants will have to sign up for Facebook if as the work is offered through the social networking site; rates of pay per each task varies, but writing tasks can pay approximately 3 cents a word. Workers will need a PayPal account in order to get paid by them. Find out

more by visiting the site at
http://www.cloudcrowd.com/how-it-works/get-started

Virtual Bee

Virtual Bee requires people for completing data entry work. People applying for this position will have to undergo an assessment and will be working as an independent contractor. Payments are made once a worker has reached a total of $30; payments are made by cheque. Applicants need to be over 18 to apply; international positions are also available. I've been advised the application process is a lengthy one and it can take several weeks before you'll hear back.

https://workers.virtualbee.com/home/about/

Music Magpie

This isn't a work from home opportunity, but it is still a chance to make some extra money from the CDs and DVDs that don't get listened to or watched anymore. You'll need to have at least 10 items to sell and the barcodes need to be entered in to see what they are worth. The advantage with this site is that there is no need to pay postage as they will send out a label, but the CDs/DVDs will have to be dropped off at a collection point. It's worth checking if it is possible to get more for your CDs and DVDs from Music Magpie before listing them on eBay and Amazon.

NOTES

Forums

We Love Forums

We Love Forums pay 10 - 25 cents per post. Payments are made via PayPal once the work has been completed. Posts have to be at least 25 words long and must adhere to all of the terms and conditions set out in order to receive payment. The board was down for maintenance work at the time of writing, but further information is available by going to http://www.weloveforums.com/write-for-us.php

Post Loop

Post Loop pays people to contribute to forums. Forum posters have to write ten trial posts so they can assess the standard of the post and if the application is approved then writers can start signing up for forums and get paid for contributing to them. Forum posters earn points for each post and once the poster has reached 100 points, they can be redeemed for $5.00 via PayPal. Earnings add up reasonably quickly and it is easy to reach payment without too much effort.

www.postloop.com

Kick Start Your Forums

This site was actively hiring at the time of writing this. Applicants need to fill out a short form and they will send you the details you need get started. Forum posters will have to complete some trial posts before they can start to undertake paid work.

http://www.kickstartyourforums.com/portal/hiring.php

Wired Flame

To get started with Wired Flame writers need to set up an account and fill out an application form. Once the account has been approved forum posters can then start earning 0.15 for a post and 0.12 for a thread. There is a limit to how many posts/threads writers can start a day and writers must adhere to these rules. Payments are made via PayPal.

http://www.wiredflame.com/

NOTES

ARTICLE WRITING

Before I get started on article writing, it is worth pointing out that article writing work can often be found through sites like ProBlogger or Craig's List. There are also a number of freelance sites around such as Elance that all offer freelance writing work. As always, writers should be careful when applying to adverts online and ensure they are genuine before carrying out work for people.

Article Document US ONLY

Article Document is open to US contractors; they pay monthly via PayPal. Unlike some sites, writers aren't asked to write a predetermined amount of articles every week or month. However, writers do need to write an article at least once every 90 days for their account to remain active. Pay rates aren't given, but will be dependent on the kind of work carried out. Further details can be found by visiting them at:

http://www.articledocument.com/

Triond

No one is going to get rich writing for Triond - or for any of the smaller content writing sites - but Triond is one still worth including on the list. Page views are down since the Panda algorithm change so most page views come from Triond itself. With less page views, come falling ad revenues so with the way it pays out these days, writers are unlikely to make more than a few cents per article. However, once published on Triond, it can then be republished on some of the other content sites. Finding a niche and writing around that is a good idea when writing for sites like Triond. For example, if a writer were to choose health or cooking/recipes as their niche, then these articles could be compiled into a book to maximise income.

www.triond.com/

Hubpages

Hubpages allows its users to publish articles in the form of *Hubs* and gives users a number of options to earn from them. To earn revenue from views, the writer will need an AdSense account. Alternatively, there is the option to earn from Amazon sales. As with other writing sites, a writer would need a large number of hubs before they could start making good money, but I've seen a number of people doing just that.

Hubpages.com/

Squidoo

Squidoo is similar to Hubpages in that it offers multiple ways to earn from the articles that are posted. They call the articles *Lens* and writers can earn from on page advertisements and affiliate links such as Amazon and eBay. The site has a low pay out level of just $1 and payments are made via PayPal. I have seen some writer's state that they earn $1000 a month, while others have yet to earn anything. Like most writing sites, earnings are dependent on the effort put in, but the best thing to do is to write and to learn how the site works first before worrying about income. Find them at www.squidoo.com

Yahoo! Voices

Yahoo! Voices has sites in both the US and the UK. Writers can write on a range of subjects from cooking and news stories to sports and creative writing. With these types of sites people need a large collection of articles before they'll start earning a good income, so bear this in mind when starting out. Payments are $1.50 or £1.50 per 1000 views and payments are made via PayPal. There is also the chance to earn from upfront payments.

http://voices.yahoo.com/

Textbrokers

TextBrokers are looking for writers in the UK and the United States. If a writer wants to work for them they need to fill out a short application form and then write a sample article of at least 120 words. TextBrokers will give a list of subjects to write about and the writer can choose one from the list. It's best to write your sample piece off the site, and then copy it into the box provided, then if the writing sample is not received properly then it can be resubmitted without writing it out twice.

In order to verify your application, applicants might be asked for Photo ID. If you don't have Photo ID or a Driving License, or don't wish to share it, then advise them you don't have a picture ID and they can verify your account over the phone.

www.textbroker.co.uk or www.textbroker.com

London Brokers

London Brokers are looking for people to write content for them. The application process is easy and once your application has been accepted then writers can begin to have a look at the type of work the site has available. Writers get paid $2.00 -$6.50 an article and the amount earned will vary depending on your experience. Payments are made weekly and can be made via PayPal or Payoneer. Find out more at:
http://www.londonbrokers.net/payment.php

Digital Journal

Digital Journal is a Canadian based news site that pays its writers for news articles. The minimum pay-out is $10 via PayPal and payments are made on the first of every month. Earnings have a tendency to move up and down, but by writing articles that attract a lot of votes and page views it is possible to do well out of this. Find out more at http://www.digitaljournal.com

Quality Gal US ONLY

Quality Gal is seeking writers from the US. The site states that they pay $15 for an article and that people signing up with them must provide a photo I.D as a form of identification. Payments are sent via PayPal each Friday or a check option for payment is also available. The application details can be found at:

http://www.qualitygal.com/writer-application

Writer's Access US ONLY

Writer's Access are looking for US-based writers for content writing work. Writers get paid monthly via PayPal and rates of pay will depend on your star rating. I don't know much about this site, but it does seem to have some good feedback. Find out more at:
http://www.writeraccess.com/

Expertscolumn

Expertscolumn enables its writers to earn a passive income from their articles. Writers need to accumulate a large quantity of articles before they can start making a reasonable income, but with hard work and dedication you'll notice a steady increase in your earnings every day. I have been paid several times from time and have found them to be reliable. Payments are made once you have earned $5.00. Some people earn enough to cash out every day, I don't have enough articles to do that yet, but I am working on it. Expertscolumn has recently introduced a paid to comment aspect to the site, which seems to be working well. Expertscolumn recently announced they won't be paying their writers, but it is hoped the signed can continue in a new format.

NOTES

STOCK PHOTOS

In recent years, stock photo sites have become increasingly popular. There are many sites around but experts would advise starting out with just a few of them. Photographers only license there designs to these sites, although there is the option to sell exclusive rights to some sites. Photographers always retain the copyright so contributors can also use their pictures on design sites like Cafepress or Zazzle.

Adherence to the guidelines is the most important thing when getting photographs accepted. It's worth visiting the sites, looking at the bestselling categories and taking it from there. It is also important to read the terms and conditions carefully.

Some people take a range of pictures to see what sells while others specialise; you need to do what works for you. I've seen some photographer's state that they earn $1000 a year from one site and several hundred a year from other sites. Not a fortune, but enough extra money to make a difference - and some people earn thousands of dollars from just one picture.

Don't be fooled into thinking that selling your pictures is an easy way to make a living. Each of the pictures will have to be to the required standards and you'll need plenty of downloads before you can earn anything from them.

Shutterstock

Shutterstock pay 0.25 - $75.00 per image. They can use all sorts of images including abstracts, beauty and fashion shots, food and drink, health etc. Minimum pay-out is $75 via PayPal or Moneybookers and $300 via cheque. Residents in the US need to fill out a W9 form and if you live outside the US then you'll need to fill out a W-8 form for tax purposes or 30% of your earnings can be withheld.

http://submit.shutterstock.com/?language=en

Picture Nation

Picture Nation allows users to offer their photographs for license. Photographers get 40% commission on all pictures sold and photographers keep the copyright of their images so they can be sold on to other stock photography sites as well. Looking at the 'images we need' section will give a good idea of what the site is looking for. There is also a section detailing the kind of pictures they can't use, so you'll need to have a look at that, too. Payments are made once the pay-out level of £50.00 has been reached and payments are made via PayPal, BACS or cheque. The site can be found at: http://www.picturenation.co.uk/static/index/sell_index

IStock

Photographers need to join IStock photo before they can begin contributing photographs. Once signed up as a contributor then there is a quick quiz to complete and photographers need to upload three sample pictures. Payments are made once contributors have made $100 and can be received via cheque, PayPal, Moneybookers, direct deposit or by a pre-paid I Stockphoto Visa card. There are more details on payment royalties at the following link: http://www.istockphoto.com/help/sell-stock/about-royalties

Bigstock

Contributors need to complete a tutorial before they can begin uploading pictures. Once the tutorial has been completed and pictures have been submitted, the pictures will be reviewed, and if the pictures can be used they'll be added to the site and be made available for download; photographers will then earn commissions on any downloads. Photographers qualify for payment once they've earned $30. http://www.bigstockphoto.com/sell-your-images.html

Dreamstime

Dreamstime accept photographs and illustrations and pay out once the $100 pay-out level has been reached. Photographers can choose to receive their payment either by cheque, PayPal or Moneybookers. The photographer/artist will receive a 20-50% of revenue share of each sale made and there are bonuses if your images are exclusive. To get started, photographers just need to fill out the application and send some sample pictures. If they are accepted then the pictures will be added to the database. If the pictures are not accepted, then the photographer will be sent an email to explain why; the pictures can be resubmitted when the required changes have been made.
http://www.dreamstime.com/sellimages

Fotolia

Fotlia have a large range of categories to sell pictures under, including people, nature, etc. To get started, photographers need to sign up for an account and then they can add images and add tags to their files. To sign up, users need to be aged 18 or over and own the copyright to the pictures they submit. Find out more by visiting: http://en.fotolia.com/Info/Contributors/GeneralInformation

FOAP

FOAP is a site where people can sell their photos, but with a bit of a difference. FOAP buy photos taken from an iPhone and photographers need to download the free app to be able to contribute. For each photo sold, photographers will earn $5.00 and the same pictures can be sold time and time again. Photographers can cash out via PayPal. Before getting started, it is important to read the FAQ section first: http://foap.com/pages/faq.

Scoopshot

Scoopshot are also looking for pictures; photographers need an iPhone to upload them. The company can also use pictures from some android devices. Like FOAP, users need to download the free app before they can submit pictures. Scoopshot can also use video footage. Again, it is important to read through the FAQs to understand exactly how the company works and what kind of material they can use. http://www.scoopshot.com/faq/

NOTES

MARKET RESEARCH

Saros Research

Saros Research are looking for people to take part in part-time market research work. This is open to UK residents only and pays £30-£100 for two hours of your time. In return for the money, participants would be required to take part in group discussions, product testing or interviews. With this type of work, participants might have to travel and might find that the work isn't very consistent, but it's extra money and this is a well-established company.
http://www.sarosresearch.com/Choosing-to-apply.html

Ipsos Mori

Ipsos Mori are looking for people from throughout the UK to carry out face-to-face market research. Interviewers will usually be required to travel to training for this, but pay is quite good and interviewers get a mileage allowance for travelling. Anyone who wants to work for Ipsos Mori needs to work three days a week, have access to a car and landline telephone, and be free weekends and evenings. Find out more by going to
http://www.ipsos-mori.com/careers/facetofaceinterviewers.aspx

One Poll

One Poll are more like a survey company, but the web page describes them as a market research company. Participants will be paid for taking part in online surveys; payments are made in the form of cash prizes or payments via a PayPal account. They state that surveys are offered daily and they also have a free iPhone app so people can even earn while they are on the move.

http://www.onepoll.com/sign-up

Focus4people

Focus4people carry out focus groups in the UK. When I checked I could not find out the details of pay, but this should be made available to people when they are notified of a focus group. They have an application form to fill out, which can be found at:

http://www.focus4people.com/system/register.asp

Indiefield

Indiefield carry out online and postal surveys and also employ interviewers throughout the UK for fieldwork. To find out their current requirements, visit the website and then use the contact button at the top of the page. http://www.indiefield.co.uk/fieldwork/index.html

NatCen

NatCen for Social Research have vacancies in the UK for freelance interviewers. Interviewers would need to be able to drive, be able to use a laptop, and have a broadband connection. Interviewers would have to work around 20 hours a week and the work involves face-to-face interviews.

They do have other vacancies but these are in specific areas so you'd need to live locally. It is worth visiting the site and seeing what is available.

Rates of pay are not given online. The application form can be found at: http://www.natcen.ac.uk/about-us/job-opportunities/freelance-interviewers

NOTES

FREELANCE SITES

People Per Hour

People Per Hour allows workers to apply for work online and bid on projects. Workers are employed on a freelance basis. There are a number of ways of applying for work and attracting clients such as the ability to search for jobs and then send a proposal to the perspective employer. The People Per Hour system makes it easy to apply for work and track clients and invoice them via the website. As well as applying for work online, users of the site can also advertise their skills and attract projects that way.

www.peopleperhour.com/

Odesk

Odesk offers a wide range of work from article writing and blog content writing to web site design and much more. Before a freelancer can get started, freelancers will need to fill out a profile and there is also a series of tests a freelancer will need to fill out if they want to increase their chances of finding work. Find out more at: http://www.odesk.com

Elance

Elance is one of the best known freelance sites and it is easy to get started with. All that needs to be done in order to bid for projects is to register and fill out a profile. Freelancers might also have to complete some tests depending on the type of work you're looking for. It is free to join. However, free membership will limit the amount of projects a freelancer can bid on.

Paid subscriptions are also available. Paid subscriptions will allow users to bid on more projects, but new users to the site who want to test it out might find the unpaid options are best to begin with.

www.elance.com/

Ifreelance

Ifreelance has many work from home projects to bid on. Once signed up, freelancers can choose from anything from editing and writing work to graphic design and photography. When I looked there was plenty of opportunities available and plenty of data entry work available for those interested in that type of work. http://www.ifreelance.com/?gclid=CIXvvIOSjLcCFSXLtAod 2AANQ

Guru.com

Guru.com is easy to sign up for, but there is quite an extensive profile to fill out, which is worth doing as the better the profile, the better chances of being successful in finding work. I've signed up for the site, but I haven't yet had time to bid on too many projects. The site often contacts its registered users with suitable projects via email, so that saves time trawling through the site every day. I have found the site easy to use and it seems well-suited towards beginners.

http://www.guru.com/index.aspx?gclid=CKbl1YqTjLcCFUX JtAod4iYAoQ

NOTES

NOTES

PAID SEARCH

Most of us go online every day to search for something, but many people don't realise they could get rewarded for searching. Most of the sites I have found do not pay cash directly, but they pay in the form of points that can be exchanged for PayPal payments, vouchers, gifts etc. If the vouchers come in paper form, then these can be sold on if the terms and conditions allow. I often sell on £10.00 vouchers and can get £8.00 upwards for them. Some people also sell on the free gifts they claim. For instance, some people choose video games and sell these on because the mark up is good. However, prizes can sometimes vary so they might not always be available. Some sites also pay in Amazon vouchers, which can be saved up to pay for gifts or for paying for household items, which is what I do.

The first site I would recommend is www.swagbucks.com. The site gives users many opportunities to earn aside from daily searches. Users of the site can earn from watching videos, taking part in daily polls, surveys etc. I've been paid by them several times and they are always quick at sending out prizes and payments

Irazoo

Irazoo is another site that will pay people to search; users of the site can also get paid for watching videos. playing games, filling out surveys and completing offers. Like Swagbucks, this site won't earn people a lot of money, but it is all extra cash, and it is free. Rewards are given in cash and these can then be exchanged for prizes, including PayPal payments. You'll need to be a member of

Facebook or know someone who is as this site is by invitation only.

http://www.irazoo.com/

Zoombucks

Zoombucks also pays for searches, playing games etc. Participants are paid in points and once they've reached 650 points, these can be exchanged for a $5.00 PayPal payment. www.zoombucks.com

MOCK JUROR JOBS US ONLY

When I was searching for paid work that I could do from home, I discovered some mock jury sites. Unfortunately for me, the ones I found were only available to people in the US so if you are based in the States, then mock juries are an interesting opportunity to get involved in.

Online Verdict

Online Verdict need people in the US to take part in mock juries. Applicants need to be based in the US and have to be aged 18 or over. The site does not state how regular the work will be, but when I visited the site they were currently recruiting. Jurors get paid $60 - $200 for taking part. and can choose which cases they want to review and which cases they don't.
http://www.onlineverdict.com/jurors.php

Ejury

Ejury also offer opportunities to US citizens who want to take part in mock juries. Applicants have to be over 18, based in the US and not have been convicted of a felony. They don't guarantee cases, and when I looked I couldn't find details on pay. To sign up go to:

http://www.ejury.com/jurors_signup.html

Jury Test

Jury Test also require online jurors. There is a short application form that can be filled out online and a juror agreement that will have to be read through before signing up with them. The application form can be found at http://www.jurytest.net/index.cfm?action=signupjur or to find out more about Jury Test before signing up visit: http://www.jurytest.net/index.cfm?action=aboutus

Trial Juries

Trial Juries also have opportunities for mock jurors. The site states that it pays $30 for approximately an hours work, but more complicated cases will pay more; this is payable via PayPal. Again, applicants have to be over 18 and reside in the United States. Find out more about them by visiting the FAQ http://www.trialjuries.com/trialjuries/faq.html and to sign up, visit http://www.trialjuries.com/trialjuries/signup.html

NOTES

PAID TO BLOG

There are many sites out there that will pay people to blog. Bloggers get paid a set amount per post; most of the companies pay via PayPal. Each site has its own set of terms and conditions. Some require that your blog has a certain amount of traffic every day before they'll let a blogger sign up with them, while others ask that the blog is updated regularly and that the blog has been established for a set length of time

Pay Per Post

Pay Per Post have been around for seven years. Bloggers have to earn $50.00 to be able to cash out. The price per word is set up as 0.3 cents so bloggers will earn $6.00 for a 200 word post; there is the option of charging extra for paid links.

https://payperpost.com/bloggers/blogger-how-it-works/

Payu2blog

Payu2blog pays bloggers for carrying out assignments. Payments are made via PayPal and are made within 14 days of writing the blog post. Not every blog will be accepted as part of the programme. Bloggers lucky enough to get their application accepted are not obliged to do a set amount of blog posts.

http://www.payu2blog.com/blogger-faq.htm

Sponsored Reviews

Sponsored Reviews are looking for bloggers. They state that many of their bloggers make an extra $50 a week, while others make much more. Applicants will need to have an established blog with at least 10 blog posts. The blog should also be 90 days old at the very least. Each blog registered must also be registered with search engines. Payments are made via PayPal within two weeks of completing the blog posts.

http://www.sponsoredreviews.com/page/get-paid-to-blog.html

ContentBLVD US ONLY

ContentBLVD are looking for bloggers. The application process is much tougher than with some other sites, but the pay is also much better with the site stating that it will pay $12-$48.00. Applicants need to live in the United States and work is done on spec. Articles also have to be 600 words or more. ContentBLVD also offer free content to blog owners, but this only applies if a blog has a page rank of 2 or more. https://www.contentblvd.com/how-it-works/how-to-get-paid-to-write

NOTES

64

TRANSLATION WORK

If you can speak a second language fluently, then you can earn some extra money as a translator. The years of experience a translator will need will vary from company to company, with some requiring more experience than others. Some sites ask people to carry out an assessment first and if is completed successfully, then they'll add the translator to the company's database and they'll be contacted when work is available. If your knowledge of a second language is limited then Amazon's Mechanical Turk is a good idea. They often have tasks available that involve translating just a few sentences, and it is a good way of building your confidence and skills

Global Voices

Global Voices are looking for both translators and interpreters. There is a short application form to fill out and applicants can state their rate per 1000 words. The application form can be found by going to: http://www.globalvoices.co.uk/work-for-us/translator-application.php

Translation Express

Translation Express are inviting applicants. The form is more complex than the one found on Global Voices, and they ask for quite a lot of information, including a CV. The application form can take up to 20 minutes to complete; I couldn't find information about the rates of pay.

http://www.translationexpress.co.uk/jobapplication.html

Gengo

Gengo are looking for translator. Anyone interested in this work much first complete a test and applicants will be given three opportunities to pass it. Once an applicant has passed the test - and got the results - translators can then begin to take on translation work: http://gengo.com/translator-team/become-a-translator/

Universal Translation

Universal Translation are currently open to applications. While they seek people who can speak all languages, they have a specific need for Danish, Finnish, Swedish and Norwegian translators. Interested applicants can visit the following link to find out more: http://www.universal-translation-services.com/translators-wanted/

NOTES

NOTES

68

WEBSITE USABILITY TESTING

Usertesting.com

Usertesting.com will pay people for testing websites. Each test will pay $10.00 and testers would have to use an on screen tester recorder as part of the testing. The company also has a requirement for mobile testers so applicants can also apply to tests sites using an android or iPhone etc. Tests typically take twenty minutes. Further information is available at:
http://www.usertesting.com/be-a-user-tester

Analysia

Analysia pay $10 for completing a 15-minute website usability test. Users are notified via email when work is available and payments are made via PayPal. In order to carry out an assessment, users will require a microphone.
http://www.analysia.com/user.asp

ProductivityEnchament.com

Productivtiyenchancement.com offers up to $50 for usability testing and the tests usually take around 30 minutes to complete. The company is open to people of all ages, but it is US-based so as with other companies, they might not employ people outside the United States.
http://www.productivityenhancement.com/usability_test
_participant.htm

Whatusersdo

Whatusersdo.com invites global participants to take part in website usability testing. The company pays in pounds, euros and dollars and each test pays eight pounds, euros or dollars. The company pays via PayPal and each test should take around twenty minutes. In order to sign up, users need to fill out a short registration form and then complete a sample test.

http://whatusersdo.com/panel/?mode=join

NOTES

ART AND CRAFT

When I first started searching the Internet in the early 2000s for opportunities to sell my art and crafts, I found that the opportunities were extremely limited. However, in recent years the popularity of selling your own craft and art work has increased dramatically and there are now many more ways to sell handmade goods.

Some people do well selling their creative works on eBay, but I found the sales there unsteady when it came to handmade goods and I presume the people who do the best are the ones that build a following for their work or who list lots of designs and increase their chances of making a sale that way.

Another thing to take into consideration is that most people won't go on eBay to search for handmade goods, and a lot that do get sold are likely found by chance. That does not mean that people shouldn't try to sell their handmade goods on eBay, though, as any extra sales add up.

Etsy

Etsy allows people to sell their homemade goods and has also introduced a section for people to sell their supplies. Opening a shop on Etsy is free and listing an item costs just 20 cents; if an item is sold then the seller will be charged 3.5% of the selling price. There is a huge range of categories to choose from such as home ware, jewellery, soaps and art, so there should be category to suit everyone.

As with any other site, the key to selling on Etsy is promoting your store and getting your name out there. There are some links to help with this in the resources chapter.

http://www.etsy.com

Folksy

Folksy is a UK-based website that allows people to sell their handmade items. The site has everything from cards and stationary to art, clothing, jewellery and home ware. Folksy is free to join and listing costs just 15p an item plus VAT. Items will be listed on Folksy for 120 days, or until they are all sold. There is a 6% commission fee on all sold items and membership upgrades are also available. Sellers can receive their payments via PayPal.

http://folksy.com/

Notonthehighstreet

Not on the high street is another way of selling your unique handmade items. They are looking for UK-based sellers who make items that are not readily available elsewhere; sellers need to complete an application to be considered as a partner. Successful applicants will have to pay a membership fee in order to sell their products on the site. Further information is available by visiting: http: www.notonthehighstreet.com

Imagekind

Imagekind allows artists and photographers to sell their images as prints and earn a commission on sales. There are no sign up fees for getting started and once a seller has opened an account, they can start to add their artwork. The home page gives a good idea of what other people are making and of what is selling. The site also has a strong community, which is worth looking at. Joining in some of the discussions will help to gain a greater understanding of the site. Sellers retain the copyright to their items, so sellers can also list the items on other sites.

http://www.imagekind.com/sell/art-photography.aspx

SALES

Selling isn't for everyone, but earning from party plan or selling from catalogues can earn a steady income. I used to sell Avon; I managed to build up a regular round of people to sell to as well as selling to family and friends. Some people do make full time businesses out of such opportunities, but even if the business is on part time or on an occasional basis, then the extra income can add up.

Vie at Home

Virgin are looking for people to work as a consultant selling their products on a commission basis. As well as selling skincare, make up and body care products, Virgin also sell Pierre Lang jewellery, perfumes and diet products. If someone hosts a party, then they have the potential to earn free products.

http://www.myvirgincosmetics.com/work-from-home/join_us.asp

Jamie at Home

Jamie at Home offers the opportunity to earn 20% of commission on products sold through party plan. There is a fee for buying the starter kit, which costs £120.00; a smaller kit is available for £70.00. Earnings will obviously vary, but the site states that people can earn approximately £50.00 in commission from each party. People also have the opportunity to become a Team Leader or Manager.

https://www.jamieathome.com/make-money/manager-opportunities.html

Usborne Books

Usborne Books is well-established and offers the opportunity to earn from selling children's books via party plan, school events and book fairs. There is an opportunity to build a team and the start kit, which includes books and stationary, is affordable at £38 at the time of writing. Another good thing about Usborne is the support offered to organisers. If someone signs up, then they will be assigned a mentor to help them build their business.

http://www.usbornebooksathome.co.uk/

Mary Kay Cosmetics

Mary Kay Cosmetics offers a range of online, print and mobile tools to enable consultants to run their business. Mary Kay Cosmetics also sell jewellery, body care and fragrances and sellers have the chance to earn up to 50% in commission. A starter kit needs to be purchased. There are two sites: http://www.marykay.com/en-US/BeABeautyConsultant/Pages/Default.aspx

http://www.marykay.co.uk/page/money-rewards

Avon

It used to be that Avon was a door to door business, but now Avon representatives will get their own web page as well and can earn commissions from the products sold online. For more information visit; http://www.uk-representatives.co.uk/?gclid=CP6H9cCDk7cCFZMftAodVhsAHA

Phoenix Trading

Phoenix Trading sells cards, stationery and gift wrap. This is another well-established company and the start-up pack is also affordable at £30.00. No minimum orders are required, but there is a charge for postage.
https://www.phoenix-trading.co.uk/web/corp/area/sales/?bid=84788efb0ee36e6dd4be185564332532bbd8fbb2

OTHER WAYS OF EARNING

There are obvious ways of earning extra money online such as eBay, Amazon and other online marketplaces.

There is no need to buy wholesale when starting out on eBay. Carboot sales and charity shops are good for buying low priced, quality items that can be sold on for profit.

Alternatively, offer a service like babysitting or dog walking or create your own unique products and sell those on eBay or Amazon.

RESOURCES:

Transcription

http://www.totalrecorder.com/

http://express-scribe.en.softonic.com/

Virtual Assistants

http://www.societyofvirtualassistants.co.uk/

http://www.iava.co.uk/

http://allianceofukvirtualassistants.org.uk/

Translation:

http://www.atc.org.uk/

Mystery Shopping

http://www.mspa-eu.org/en/

Craft

http://etsianartists.blogspot.co.uk/p/promote-your-etsy-shop.html

http://www.etsy.com/teams/13926/promote-your-shop-off-of-etsy-with-free/discuss/11005247/

http://www.artbusiness.com/webworks.htm

Direct Sales/Party Plan

http://dsa.org.uk/index.phpl

NOTES

NOTES

This book will be updated on a regular basis. If you have any feedback for the book or know of a work from home opportunity you'd like mentioned then please contact me.

Jane Fazackarley is the author of the forthcoming novel *Then he left me* and the owner of the jfnews.co.uk website. If you have a story you'd like to share or would like to contribute, then please contact me on jane.fazackarley@gmail.com

www.ingramcontent.com/pod-product-compliance
Lightning Source LLC
Chambersburg PA
CBHW071612170526
45166CB00003B/1062